Modern Mythology

poems about gods, mortals, and monsters

Nadia McGhee

Mythos
(n.) a myth or mythology

Table of Contents

I. The Primordial Age

"In the beginning, there was nothing
Then Chaos took a breath
And cosmos formed"

Chaos was the first to exist
She is the Mother Goddess of Creation
Every galaxy you could ever find is hers
Every creature is hers alone
Which means you, darling
You are beautifully made of chaos
You are uncontrollable and wild
Galaxies breathe as you do

Chaos

I am the primordial Goddess
The first God to ever exist
I am the dark, mysterious majesty
And the cosmos were my gift

In the beginning, there was only me
There was no light and no sound
I was free, wild, and untamable
Not even to time was I bound

I hold the ever-expanding space in my hands
When I laugh, galaxies come alive
Once you have had a taste of Chaos
You will never have anything as divine

I am the primordial Goddess Chaos
The one true creator of everything
You could try to fit my existence into words
But you will never fully understand me

Chaos to Nyx

Chaos once whispered to Nyx

"you are my daughter,
born from my power alone,
never let anyone disrespect your birthright"

The Night Goddess

I am the night triumphant
The sweet darkness is mine alone
And it is in the silent shadows
That I have made myself at home

Shadows swirl around me
Bowing to their Queen of the Night
People may fear my darkness
But I also bring beautiful light

I am the stars eternal
I fill the night sky with stars
I have breathtaking constellations
That race along my arms

I am the darkness and the starlight
I have powers the world has never seen
I am the Goddess of the Night
Even the King of the Gods fears me

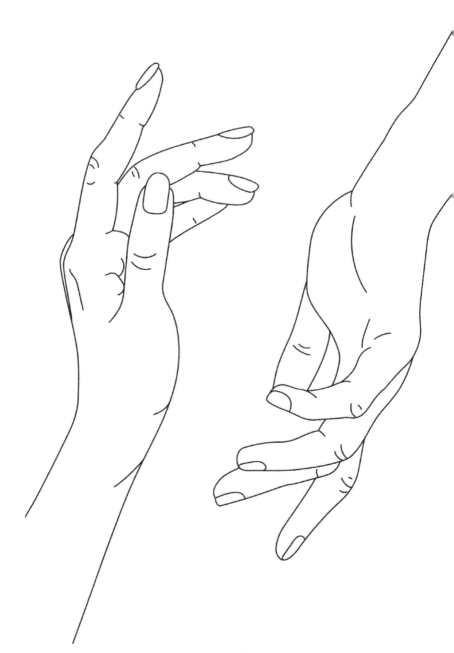

6

Erebus Whispers

How should I love you, my dear?

Love me for my darkness
Because it loves yours
Connect the stars on my skin
With your searing kiss
Love me
Not because I am full of light and luster
But because I am an arcane Goddess
And my mysterious night
Will keep pulling you in
For all eternity

Gaea

From the expanding cosmos of Chaos
Gaea was the first to arrive
She was a beautifully wild Goddess
The mother of creation and life

She breathed and the wind would blow
It was her hiccups that made hills rise
The world was hers to create
And the joy could be seen in her eyes

With her hands, she painted flowers
Made each daisy and rose unique
She clapped and mountains would grow
With ever-rising peaks

With a gentle sigh, she made forests
Full of bright lights and glowing green
With her anger, she sparked volcanoes
And those eruptions destroyed everything

When she let out her bright laugh
Birds on soft wings were formed
And wolves with sharp, gleaming teeth
Were created whenever she swore

Her eyes would remind you of a doe
But she had canines in her smile
Yes, Gaea was formed from Chaos
And she will always be devastatingly wild

Creating Uranus

Gaea created the earth
In all its wondrous majesty
She made rolling hills and sharp mountains
She formed animals of all shapes and sizes
Gaea is the creator of life

But she had no one to share it with
No one who would love her majesty
The way it should be loved

So Gaea reached up
And with her life creating hands
She created the sky
Named him her equal
Her love
Her Uranus

How the Earth Loved the Sky

Let me tell you the tale
Of how the Earth loved the Sky
She made mountains tall enough to reach him
And birds that could soar that high

Oh how Creation loved him
But she knew how to love herself first
And when the Sky angered her
Volcanoes would rage as she cursed

The Beginning of a Prophecy

My son came to me one day
And told me he wanted to be king
I did not know he would end my reign
Or that a prophecy would start with me

It starts with sons dethroning their fathers
Fighting for their chance at the throne
Wars will rage across continents
As royal bloodlines are overthrown

I started this horrible tradition
I was the first to fall from the sky
The Gods may be powerful beings
But even we have darkness inside

I remember that fateful day
When Kronos cut me down with his scythe's swing
I looked him dead in the eyes and said
"One day, your son will be king"

The Birth of Hemera and Aether

One day Darkness spoke out to the Night
And the beautiful Nyx laid in the dark embrace
As the Bright Day was born
Along with the Heavenly Light

darkness brings the most beautiful things

The Cycle of Day and Night

Every evening, the powerful Nyx
Draws her dark veil across the sky
The earth welcomes her dark embrace
And falls asleep to her nightly lullaby

When Helios drives the sun from the horizon
Hemera rises to bring the day
She disperses her mothers dark mists
And puts her stunning beauty on display

They work in a never-ending routine
Only meeting at dusk and dawn
Hemera allows the sun to shine
While Nyx guides stars to wish upon

Nyx brings the heavenly darkness
Hemera bathes the earth in a soft light
And together the Goddesses work
Through their endless cycle of day and night

Questions for the Fates

You are the great daughters of Nyx
And I have questions for you
You dictate the lives of everyone
But in the end what do you lose?

You are the spinner, Clotho
The beginning of life is in your hands
Are you starting to grow weary
Of weaving lives into little strands?

Lachesis, the one who measures
They call you the decider of destinies
How do you pick the lengths of life?
Do you choose them carefully?

You are the ender of life, Atropos
The sister who cuts the string
Do you shed tears for every thread
That you cut on your tapestry?

Clotho, Lachesis, Atropos
The Moirai, the Three Fates
Balancing life and death is hard
But is that not why you share the weight?

Being Nyx

I never fit the mold of a Goddess
The darkness was always my home
I wasn't light laughs and soft silk
I was night skies and broken thrones

My mother, Chaos, taught me better
I learned to embrace the hidden parts of me
She knew I was too dark for other Gods
And that I was more than they would ever be

Maybe that is why I never loved Olympus
It was always too perfect, too bright
And I am both beauty and darkness
I am Nyx, the Goddess of the Night

Understanding Chaos

Can you describe chaos?

Some may say *it's destruction*
Others will tell you *it's confusion*
And there will be those who offer you *a law of science*

But can you encapture the entirety of a Goddess
The first Goddess
The first primordial being
Into simple words?
Words that allow the human mind
To understand her?

You can try
But you will not succeed

II. The Titan Age

"In Unity with the Sky
Gaea bore 12 Golden Gods
Uranus called them Titans Theoi
The Straining Gods"

The Memory of Eurynome

You were a queen once Eurynome
But your story was lost to history
Now your name is scarcely mentioned
And you have become a mystery

You are a lost legend
In time, the world has forgotten your name
But there are some who remember you
And the height of your glorious reign

The Birth of the Titans

I think there was a moment when we were happy
A family not corrupted by greed
I remember when I gave birth to the Titans
My perfect, golden children
As I basked in the glow of afterbirth
Uranus came to me
And he whispered
You are a remarkable thing
Everything that comes from you
Is beautiful and flawless
And I smiled up at him
Until I saw the look in his eyes
Staring at our children
Who were growing fast
As young Gods and Goddesses do
And a thought came
As fleeting as the wind
What if they weren't beautiful?
What if they weren't flawless?
Would you still love them?
Would you still love me?
But then the thought became background noise
And I forgot about it

I wish I ran that day

24

Giving Birth to Monsters

As a mother, you love your children
You hold them close and keep them safe
But giving birth to monsters
Ties them to a horrible fate

Your husband begins to blame you
Because your children are not perfect
So he tosses them down the great chasm
Before you can even object

You are angry now
And soon the world will feel your wrath
You will become an earthquake
Bringing down everyone in your path

So you may have given birth to monsters
But you have great things planned
For you have also given birth to Titans
And your husband will fall by their hands

The Fall of the Cyclops

When your mother gave birth to you
Her fears came true
You were a challenge to your father
To his perfect image
You were not perfect enough
To become figurines in his palace
You tried to win your fathers favor
You created weapons fit for kings
But Uranus could never love you
Your twelve elder siblings were perfect
Why weren't you?
He called you a failure
So he locked you away
Along with your brothers
And you will always remember your mother's face
The look of distraught
The look of knowing
And the anger
The anger scared you
Every evening, when night fell across the sky
She would come down to you
Whispering softly
You are the most beautiful thing I have created
You are not a monster
He is.

The Anger of Gaea

I gave Uranus love and life
But he hated the gifts that I gave
I gave him Titans and monsters
But it was only power that he craved

Uranus thought he could rule over me
So when his blood soaked the earth
I raised Titans that crushed gods like him
So he would never again doubt my worth

How to survive Titanhood
(Lessons from the Titanides)

I. Theia

You must become celestial
Give the world the sun and the moon
Then become unbreakable like a diamond
So no one can break you

II. Rhea

You find comfort in your children
And find comfort in being alone
Because you can't always trust your family
Who are all greedy for the throne

III. Themis

You see a world without order
You see chaos and despair
So you teach justice to younger generations
So the world remains balanced and fair

IV. Mnemosyne

You remember the little moments
And you preserve them in your memories
Being a Titan Goddess is challenging
So you find happiness in the little things

V. Phoebe

You learn how to become radiant
Your sister gives you the gift of prophecies
It is a burden that you will carry
But you learn to carry it with ease

VI. Tethys

You become like the water
Nurturing the soils of the world
And you learn to protect yourself from within
Like a calm protecting a pearl

Themis to Nemesis

I see the fire burning in you
We may both be justice
But you are more wrathful
Than I will ever be
You have learned
That justice and revenge
Are dishes best served cold
You were taught
To take your sword
And become the judge
And the executioner
You hand out your sentences
With your sword in hand
Swinging blindly

Being Star-like

Your kisses have fused into my skin
Along my arms, exploding stars have given birth
At night, I see your dreams and wishes
As your starry tears fall towards the earth

I whisper my secrets to your stars
Hoping they will deliver my silent prayers
Your beautiful nebulas fill the sky
As I watch with a wide-eyed stare

You are the star-touched Asteria
You form constellations with your syllables
I have seen you form new worlds with your hands
And create your exploding miracles

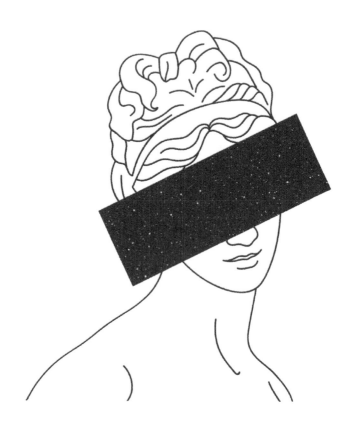

Asteria Collapsing

He chased you
To the ends of the very earth
But he will not be your destruction
No, this is your rebirth

Allow yourself to crumble Asteria
Your fate will not be one they mourn
For you are a blazing star
You must collapse before you are born

Asteria's Love Letter to Hecate

I took my stardust
Along with your father's ruination
And I fused it into your veins
At night, I whispered
The secret language of the stars
Into your bloodstream
You are magic Hecate
I gave you the power of a supernova
So you could survive the flames of life
Take my fallen majesty
And make a legacy out of it
You are destruction and fallen stars
The world is yours for the taking

Hecate

Listen to me, my sisters
For I offer you a powerful choice
I can give you power that men dream of
If you follow the sound of my voice

Hear the Latin dripping from my lips
As I curse those who have done me wrong
Listen closely as I chant spells
That sound like siren songs

They fear the power I possess
Because I could rule the world
And to men who think they're above me
I'm just a stupid, naive girl

So they will try to burn me
And they will try to burn you too
But witches are the deadliest kind of woman
Because of the fire we must walkthrough

The Island of Asteria

Zeus thought he deserved me
But Goddesses are not spoils of war
I would never belong to him
And on the river Styx, I swore

I could not let him have me
I wouldn't be a prize he got to win
So I became an island to protect myself
And the stars that reside on my skin

But your fate was not kind Leto
Trust that your trials will be over soon
On my shores, there is a haven
Where you can give birth to the sun and moon

So come to me, my sister
On my island, you can safely rest
You can hide from Hera's wrath
And finally, catch your breath

The Cries of Leto

Being hated by a Goddess
For something you didn't choose
Forces you into a game
One that you will always lose

You try to tell her you are a victim
That you and her are one and the same
Men have played the both of you
And they are the ones to blame

But she still believes in love
And she won't listen to your cries
So you must begin to run
Trying to find places where you can hide

Leto's Plight

When you give birth to the sun
The daylight becomes your enemy
Helios whispers your location in Hera's ear
And the vengeful Goddess laughs
As you try to run

When you give birth to the moon
Selene becomes your only companion
She tells you that your children will be worth it
Because you will give birth to warriors
And you smile through your tears

40

Selene Incarnate

You are a celestial being
The Arcane Goddess of the Moon
In the evening, I look upon Nyx's sky
As I listen to your mournful tune

They have forgotten your presence
Overlooked by Gods, mortals, and fate
They will sing praise to warrior Artemis
But not of the beautiful moon incarnate

Perhaps that is your binding curse
You can only be seen at night
They will compare you to the sun
But it could never shine as bright

You are a calm but mighty goddess
I have seen you move the vast seas
People may worship the Blinding Helios
But you are the Lunar Selene

Loving Helios

I once tried to love the sun
Every day, at dawn and dusk
When he was close enough to the earth
I would reach out to touch him
And his searing kiss would burn my skin
Marking his claim on my heart
But then the Night would come
And he would have to leave
So as the final streaks of light disappeared
I held my hand up
Trying to catch the last touches
Of his scorching love

Asking Atlas

What do you say to Atlas?
The Titan cursed to hold the heavens
Do you apologize for his misfortune?
Or do you bow down in his presence?

If I could, I would ask one question
For all, I want to know is why
Why does he continue to hold up the world
When he could simply let go of the sky?

Maybe it is because every night
Atlas finds peace within his fate
And as he gazes upon the fallen stars
He understands why he holds the weight

Perhaps he is tired of being a Titan
Tired of seeing death and debris
Maybe he is content, holding the world
On his starry tattooed knees

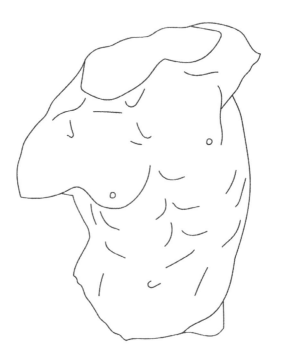

44

A Tired Titan

One night, I traced the scars on Atlas
And he whispered to me softly
"I am tired.
There are days when all I want
Is to simply let go"

I touched the stars I had kissed into his skin
Before whispering back
"Then give your world to me
So I can carry the weight with you
The heavens should not be yours alone"

Atlas Asks Prometheus

I mourn your fate, dear brother
For it is one worse than mine
You watch your creations destroy themselves
While I simply hold the sky

Maybe we are on the wrong side of history
Punished by the Gods for our sins
Are there times where you cursed their names?
When you wanted to leave the world in ruin?

Prometheus Answered

Brother, this is where we differ
Our fates both keep us restrained
But where you are an exploding volcano
I am a forgotten Titan chained

I molded mortals from clay
Gave them everything they desired
Then I was punished for them
Because I gave them the divine fire

I know you are angry, brother
With our fates, I too am frustrated
But I will not be the one to ruin
One of the things that I have created

The Earth's Lessons

As your mother, I must warn you
Rhea, do not expect love from him
Being Queen is like drowning underwater
So you must learn how to swim

Learn to become calm and timid
Keep your plans close to your heart
Every step you take must be planned
Or he will tear you apart

Play the role of the perfect wife
Place a smile upon your face
In the end, you will be the last thing he sees
Before he meets his fate

Rhea, the Actress

I watched as my husband took my children
He swallowed them in front of me
To him, I was complacent and calm
But inside, my rage ran as deep as the sea

I remembered my mother's lessons
So I stepped into the part I had to play
But I prayed for the end of the Titans
And I could not wait for that day

My husband thought I was a puppet
But a mother's love runs deep
I have played the part of the patient wife well
But in the end, it is his soul I will reap

Rhea Remembers

Will you mourn for him?
This is a fate he could not control
Did you not love him once?
When he was your husband before he was a king?

Rhea sighs.
I did love him
Before prophecies were created
And the man I loved wilted away
There was a time when I loved him
But I knew this would happen
I will mourn who he use to be
But I will not mourn who he is now

You will be the end of him

I hope I am.

The Mad King

How do you escape a prophecy?
The answer is you never do
You can try to escape it all you want
But destiny always collects its dues

You attempt to keep the prophecy at bay
So it is your children that you devour
For you know they'll be the end of you
And you will never give up your power

The rest of Titans begin to whisper
Your own wife can't look in your eyes
She starts to hate you for what you did
As she curses you while she cries

Mortals start to fear your presence
And your precious golden age is no more
Eyes watch your every move carefully
But that is something you've learned to ignore

The future will always haunt you
And it has turned you into the Mad king
Why did you try to avoid your demise?
No one ever escapes their prophecy

Titanomachy pt.1

War is not beautiful
Not like it is in the stories
As you walk among ichor drenched fields
You realize that war never brings glory

In time, these battles will have become legends
New generations rising against the old
But right now you are holding back tears of anguish
Because you had forgotten that Gods bleed gold

Fighting against your own family is crushing
The stains on your hands never leave
And the guilt you feel for hurting them
Makes it hard for you to breathe

War is not poetry
It is immortality on a fraying string
It brings the darkest question to light
Who would you kill for the chance to be king?

Titanomachy pt.2

What is a Titan King
Suppose to do
When his youngest son approaches him
Robes turned golden only by the blood of family
Demanding the throne
As he once did
To his father before him .

"Your son will overthrow you
As you have overthrown me"

Titanomachy pt. 3

War always brings consequences
No matter what side; win or lose
In the end, they will all lose something
A piece of them they never knew

Hades starts to feel like the God of Death
As he sees his family dying on the battlefield
He is fighting against his own blood
Causing wounds that will never truly heal

Demeter makes promises to herself
She will protect her future children at all costs
She wants to become something stronger
A Goddess no one will ever cross

Poseidon runs to the sea
Trying to escape his family's carnage
He tries to build a new legacy underwater
Away from the one that war has tarnished

Hestia tries to keep her family together
She continues to keep the hearth lit
But her family has been brutally broken
In ways, she refuses to admit

Hera has become queen now
And queens can never cry
But as she wipes bloodstains from her dress
Water starts to collect in her eyes

Zeus remembers bringing war to his family
So he will be the best king they ever knew
But madness runs in the veins of kings
And soon it will ruin him too

Kronos' Final Word

When your youngest son stands in front of you
Ready to cut you down
You look him in the eye
And with a broken chuckle, you say
You are the king now,
And I can only hope
That they don't turn against you
As you turned against me

III. The Olympian Age

"And with Kronos chained in Tartarus
Zeus took the sky
Poseidon took the sea
And Hades took the underworld
As a new Age of Gods rose"

A King Rising

This is a boy hiding
A mother's love protects him
A prince cast away across the sea
To be hidden from his father
So he could be safe and free

This is a prince running
He spends his days in the mountains
Hidden from his fathers searching eye
He learns to fight from his warriors
So he can dethrone the God of Time

This is a God making
He frees his sibling from their cage
Swears victory will be theirs in the end
Now a man, he stands before his father
Ready for war and hungry for revenge

This is a king rising
With a final blow, he cuts down his father
War is brutal but he has won
Now as he sits on his golden throne
A new age of Gods has begun

Metis, The Counsel of Zeus

I guess there was a time when I loved him
A time where I trusted the God-King
And for the Goddess of Cunning and Wisdom
In that moment, I was really naive

I did not see the wolfish grin upon his face
Or how he looked at me with greed
I believed every word he said
When he told me, one day I'd be queen

But one night, he crept behind me
I saw his canine smile as I cowered
He stripped the wisdom from my bones
And made sure I was fully devoured

From Metis to Hera

A king's love is a fickle thing
It comes and goes like the rain
And I hope that you fare better than I
For your fate, I can only pray

An Apology From Hera

They call me the jealous Queen
That is often how the story goes
The one who curses the innocent
While sitting on a marble throne

I use to curse them out of rage
Blaming them for my own pain
But then I realized that to kings
Women are just pawns in a game

If I had the choice, I'd leave him
I often wish for a better life to live
But I swore myself to him
And kings take but do not give

This is my apology to those girls
They're not the villain in my eyes
But how can you curse your husband
When he's the ruler of the skies?

The Fall of Hera

Hera sits in a garden alone
With a glowing smile upon her face
Her innocence revolves around her
But she does not yet know her tragic fate

Hera meets a young, handsome God
And gets caught up in his allure
Now she is queen of a golden kingdom
With a king who promises to only love her

Hera cries to her mother Rhea
To the sky, she curses Zeus' name
But then she curses herself the most
Because she allowed him to play her like a game

Hera yells at Zeus in anger
Tells him that she will leave Olympus behind
But Zeus tells her that she can never leave
And deep down, Hera knows he's right

Hera sits in a garden alone, again
Holding dead flowers, she begins to grieve
As she looks back to when she was a young goddess
And wishes she wasn't so naive

How does a God win back a Goddess?
He doesn't.

Zeus' Cry to Hera

How does a God apologize?
They fall on their blood soaked knees
And they begin to cry golden tears
As they bow before their queen

Hera, I never deserved you
I realize this now that you are gone
In chess, the queen is the most important
And yet, I treated you like a pawn

I wanted the fame and glory of being king
But now Olympus has gone cold
And I am a disgraced God by himself
Surrounded by broken pillars of marble and gold

I will only ever bow to you Hera
My crown is yours alone
You were always more powerful than me
And that is something I should have known

A Reckoning with Zeus

Zeus cries for the fate of Hera

"I destroyed her happiness
I left an innocent Goddess in ruin
I took her smile from her face
Why I was her undoing"

I laugh cruelly

"You did not destroy her
You will never have that power
She was a Queen before she had a crown
And you will always be a coward"

Hera to Hebe

My darling, let me tell you something important
Something that I wish I knew
You must always put yourself first
Even if you don't think you deserve too

You must learn how to become marble
Learn to bounce words off your skin
The world will try to break you
But you can never let them win

And Hebe, don't be afraid to break
Be the most beautiful disaster ever seen
Because you are my daughter
Which means you are a Queen

The Birth of Aphrodite

you were made from the flesh
of the old king
they chalk you up to
fairy tales
and true love kisses
but have they forgotten the stories
the true love stories
the stories of love and war
you are the reason
so many kingdoms
have burned to the ground

Goddess of ~~Love~~

I have been called a delicate Goddess
Of a silly thing called love
But they forget who I really am
About the danger in my golden blood

Instead of love, I crave destruction
Ancient power runs through my veins
The prince of Troy once asked for love
So I brought the city flames

Do not push me off as a minor Goddess
Love is a dangerous thing
I am passion, heat, and lust
You have not yet seen the destruction I bring

Men will try to tie me down
They'll call me sweetheart, baby, flower
But the world is in my hands
One day, those men will cower

"please send me love"
I asked Aphrodite one night

A satin-draped voice answered
how can I send you love,
when you refuse to love yourself?

A Memo from Aphrodite

You are a rare and untouchable beauty
And it hurts me more than you know
That you give yourself toxic love
Instead of allowing yourself to grow

You look for love in others
Before choosing to love yourself
You pick people like they are figurines
On your never-ending carousel

I know love can be destructive
I have seen the pain it's put you through
So please give yourself real love first
That is all I could ever ask of you

A Rival of Aphrodite

You have started to fear mirrors
You hate to look at them and see yourself
The rolls in your stomach that taunt you
Your stretch marks that won't go disappear
And despite all that you have done
You still don't think
You are enough
You have stared into mirrors
And have learned to hate the marks on your face
But you don't see the constellations in them that I do
You don't see the beauty that I do

I am here to tell you that a century ago
You would have been worshipped as a Goddess
A rival of Aphrodite
And you are a Goddess now
Sculptors will take in the image of you
And carve you into marble
To preserve your artistry for eternity
I ask you to love yourself
Every piece of you has been kissed by Aphrodite
And people will fight wars over your beauty

The Price of Love

Love is deadly
Tell me of Romeo and Juliet
Tell me of Eurydice and Orpheus
Tell me that love brings more pain than war
Tell me that love is destructive
Because I have only seen the harsh side of love
Tell me that heartbreak
Is more deadly
Than death.

Oh, How Beauty Loved War

Aphrodite never loved Hephaestus
But the Gods wanted her tamed
They knew how love could be weaponized
So they made sure she was restrained

Ares never loved his wars
All he brought was fear and hate
He never wanted mortals to cower from him
But war will always be his fate

Ares will always love the Goddess of Beauty
He knows that she is deadlier than she appears
At night he listens to her calls for ruin
And knows that she is something to fear

Aphrodite has always loved Ares
She knows that he is better than war
And together, they are kingdom destroyers
Something the world had never seen before

Oh darling I know it's scary
I was very scared once too
Falling in love, too quickly
Is a dangerous thing to do

The Broken God

I am violent, untamed, and insatiable
Enemies run when they heard my battle cry
I bring war, death, and carnage
But no one ever asks me why

My father made me who I am
The hated God of War
He told me that bloodshed and tragedy
Was all I was ever good for

And maybe I crave beauty
Not destruction and terrible screams
Maybe I am a broken God
Who once dreamed of pretty things

I am no Prince of Olympus
I am only praised when wars are won
So I kneel with bruised knuckles and bloody knees
Wondering when my war will be done

81

Ares Questions

Father, to you, I am a bastard
A bloodstain on your family tree
Why should I apologize to you
When you were the one who made me?

Should I ask for forgiveness?
Do you fear what I've become?
Who will carry out your bidding
If I am not the one?

Mother do you fear who I am now?
Am I too broken to walk in your palace?
You wanted a son that reminded you of yourself
But now you have one full of malice

Mother, do I scare you?
Have I made you hate the color red?
I am not your perfect Godly prince
So should you call me a monster instead?

The Loveless Blacksmith

I was never given love
when I was born, my mother
threw me off the mountain
because Gods don't give birth to monsters

I was never given love
so I built machines that had only one job
to love me as a mother should
to love me blindly

I was never given love
the Gods asked me to come home
but Olympus had always been cold to me
and my machines have always been nicer

I was never given love
they gave me a wild, beautiful Goddess
as if that would make me forget
how the Gods treated one of their own

I was never given love
so when Aphrodite sought my brother, I knew
Gods would never love anything
except what is absolutely perfect

some things just don't deserve love

The Gods are superficial

And you
you beautiful Broken boy
You tried so hard to fix yourself
So you could fit in
With the rest of your perfect family

But you are not the ugly one
They are
You have learned to create breathtaking things
From your hands
While they can only destroy beautiful things
As they have destroyed you

Hephaestus Realizes

You were beauty and self-destruction
Something I had never seen before
A mix of love and death
A woman who would ruin kingdoms
You found the beauty in being broken
And I wanted to fix you
But you loved your destruction
You craved heartbreak and love poems
I thought you were beautiful
But you destroyed things I wanted to fix
Maybe that is why we could never work
I wanted to fix what you didn't want repaired

Poseidon

I have always been a dangerous God
In my waters, you can drown
Sometimes, I am the healing water
But I can also bring kingdoms down

I have always been a changing God
I can be the calm before the storm
But then I become a raging hurricane
As I unleash my true form

I have always been the earth-shaker
Wild and unrestrained like the sea
And there were times when I made the world stop
Times when even Zeus couldn't control me

I have always been a temperamental God
There is a storm within my veins
I could drown the entire world if I wished
For I cannot be contained

you ran as far as you could
to the ends of the earth
but there is no place to run
when the ruler of the seas
wants you as his Queen

Amphitrite

When Poseidon came after me
I ran as far as I could
Because I know that Gods like him
Never love you the way they should

To him, I was a raindrop in his ocean
A pretty pearl to remain by his side
But I am the ocean at its worst
I hold a dangerous storm inside

I am the bringer of the harsh waves
That cause sailors and ships to drown
When it comes to the ruler of the seas
I am the one who wears the crown

I was never just a raindrop
I am drowned souls and sunken ships
You should never anger the Sea Goddess
Or your last breath will pass your lips

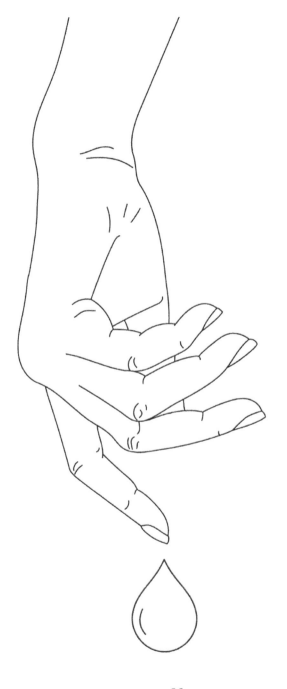

A Note from Amphitrite

you are the sea, my dear
drown your enemies
do not let them see your tears
you are so much more
than your surface
and they were foolish
for forgetting
how wonderful
how destructive
how powerful
you really are
lull the sailors to sleep, my dear
so when they awake
they will have remembered
how much you are worth

Drift

Let me drown in the ocean
Let it wash away my tears
As I drift farther from the shore
The world suddenly becomes clear

I feel the ocean's push and pull
As the water fills my eyes
It gives me such a sense of serenity
That I almost don't hear your cries

I can see you reaching for me
A tiny figure on the sandy shore
But where were you when I needed you?
When I needed you to love me more?

I hope you don't miss me too much
As I float among the waves
The ocean has pulled me in
And it will not give me away

Becoming Water

When Amphitrite was young
She learned how to become water
She learned how to become nurturing
Like the water that fills the soil
And gives life to every part of the world
She learned how to become calm
Calm enough to lull people to sleep
And wash away the worries left on her shores
She learned how to become powerful
Like the water that brings tsunamis and hurricanes
That destroy cities and drown ships
She became water

A Message from Metis

Before you were your father's weapon
Athena, you were my daughter first
Listen closely to my warnings child
Because I have seen the Gods at their worst

You carry my legacy on your shoulders
It is a weight only you can bare
You must guard yourself fiercely
And be careful with what you share

The Gods will always be watching you
Waiting for you to make a mistake and fail
So you must fight for your place Athena
And you must fight for it, tooth and nail

You will remind the Gods of my tragedy
But you will not share the same fate as I
Because where I am wisdom, you are war
And you will learn to not be kind

94

Athena of War and Wisdom

They should tell you
To fear the woman wise
It's because I am the patient one
Who hides venom in her grey eyes

I am a fierce warrior
With an even deadlier mind
You won't know what I am planning
With the facade, I hide behind

Soldiers cry out to me for guidance
Oh Athena, Goddess of Wisdom and War
When they need a deadly miracle
I am the one they pray for

I am the War Goddess
And the creator of fatal plans
I bring kingdoms crashing down
With a blood-dipped spear in hand

You remember your mother's whisper

"Your father promised I would be Queen
And lied.
But you, my daughter
You will rule
Let him trust you
But you must never trust him
You are wise Athena
One day, the throne
That was once promised to me
Will be yours
And you will be Queen"

Legacies travel generations

Asking Artemis and Athena

What does it mean to be a Virgin Goddess?
Athena's grey eyes locked on mine

"It means being wise
Gods will try to trick you
But you must be smarter
It means being warlike
So men know that trying to love you
Only results in carnage"

What if men try to harm me?
Artemis' arrows glow in the moonlight

"Then you become wild
Like the wolves that raised you
Let your teeth become red
Then you become a huntress
Draw your bow and show everyone
How exact your aim is"

Selene to Artemis

Listen to me, my little moon
For I must give you some advice
Men will fight to overshadow you
But despite this, you must rise

I know you are a wild one
But like the moon, you must be calm
The sun can have all the glory
Because the world lies in your palm

You are a wild huntress
And I swear on the River Styx
I may be the moon incarnate
But you are a solar eclipse

The Wild Goddess

You know of my twin brother
The bright God of the Sun
The one who plays music on his lyre
As poems drip from his tongue

I am the divine huntress
The one dipped in moonlight
I am the wild Goddess
Who runs with wolves at night

I am the protector of the women
That the world has tried to break
So I make them into warriors
Who burn men at the stake

And with an arrow dipped in silver
I chase away the sun-filled afternoon
I am the leader of the hunt
The deadly Goddess of the Moon

Artemis asks for the Moon

She didn't want to be a regular Goddess
When told of her fate
Artemis took to the night sky
And carved her own destiny from stardust
When her father asked her what she wanted
She did not ask for the rarest jewels
Or the prettiest ribbons
Instead, she asked him for the moon
She wanted to be magnetizing
She wanted to be eclipsing
So that even when the moon was not full
People would still feel her power

Artemis' Warning

I see her warriors spirit
But I ask do not yet teach her to fight
Let her be a child before she is a weapon
Before you corrupt her pure moonlight

Shield her from the world for now
Eventually, she will learn how to be strong
But childlike wonder is rare these days
And she won't have it for long

She is just a child
She does not need to hold the world
One day, she will lead armies
But for now, she is simply a girl

Helios to Apollo

You are a young and inexperienced God
And you haven't felt true pain
Because the sun is not yours yet
And I do not wish for that day

Being the sun God is a lonely path
You will burn too bright for love
I am sure you will try to do it anyway
But there are dangers you do not know of

Your day will come, little God
And the sun will be yours to drive
You might be an immortal being
But this is a path that few survive

The Loss of Apollo

You'd think with all the power of a God
I would be able to outrun Fate
Yes, I am the God of Light and Healing
But there are still things death can take

Hyacinth you gave me all your love
And as your blood stained the sand
I could only stand and watch
As you left me and took Death's hand

Daphne, you ran from my love
Turned yourself into a beautiful tree
Now I wear a laurel to remind myself
Of all the terror and pain that I bring

Even Gods are at the mercy of Fate
In my arms, all my lovers die
I hold them close and curse the world
As the burning sun begins to cry

Apollo Chats with Helios

Who will love the sun?

                                        why young God
                                   everyone loves the sun
                           people will dance under your light
                           and sing worship to your name

That is amazing
But that is not love
That is admiration
Who will love the sun?

                                    people will try to love you
                                     but soon they will learn
                        that the sun is untouchable for a reason
                               your fiery kiss will melt them

So the sun is lonely then?
Everyone is afraid of loving it?

                                 being the Sun God is hard
                                and no one said that this path
                              would bring happiness and joy
                           the sun is too bright, too volatile

But the sun is the center...
The center of this entire universe
Why is it lonely?

                              there is a reason why the planets
                              choose to revolve around the sun
                              they are afraid of getting too close
                              in fear that they will be burned too

Hermes, the Messenger

My mother, Maia, daughter of Atlas
Bore me as the sun broke through
Then I became the tricky messenger of the Gods
With my caduceus and golden, winged shoes

I am the one who stole Apollo's cattle
The holy animal that he acquired
But, I am the one who gifted the Sun God
With his beautiful, golden lyre

I am the messenger of the Gods
That is what the fates foretold
I am the God of Boundaries
And the deliverer of lost souls

Leopard Hearted Boy

You were not always a God
You were once a Leopard-hearted boy
But Hera's trickery took your mother
Robbing you of true love and joy

Hera's jealousy was always there
Determined to be the end of you
So now you drink to blur your mind
And forget all the pain you went through

Madness

You may be the most dangerous God, Dionysus
People fear the crazed look in your eyes
Every day, you walk between genius and insanity
And, oh, how you dance with that line

You have always hated being a God
Hera destroyed everything you ever knew
You are more human than most Olympians
Maybe that is why they fear you

Your blood is more wine than ichor
Some may call you half-human, half-god
One day, the world will dissolve into madness
And you will lift your glass and applaud

There is a reason why people fear you Dionysus
They fear the madness running through your veins
And I would hate to be there for the moment
When you lose everything that keeps you sane

110

Demeter

Olympian Gods will try to take everything
Many wanted me to be their wife
But my power is too great for them
From Gaea, I learned to master life

I decide if the earth will be plentiful
Or if every plant will die
I am as deadly as a hidden cobra
But as pretty as a butterfly

I am a mother before I am a Goddess
I live for my children alone
You dare touch a hair on their heads
Then you will see the power that I withhold

And when Persephone was stolen from me
Zeus had to beg me to end my rage
So no, I will never be an Olympian wife
I am not a toy for others to gain

From Persephone

Mother, let me tell you a secret
Your flowers always died in my hands
And I hated being the Goddess of spring
Something you could never understand

And I know how you see me
Your broken, corrupted child of light
But mother, I wanted pomegranates and death
I craved the cruel shadows of the night

Mother the God of the Dead loves me
He bows before me on his knees
He offers me a crown of thorns
And calls me his Queen

And maybe you did love me, mother
But he loves me, darkness and all
He knew that I was meant for more
Than being your silly, fragile doll

Demeter's Reply

When he stole you, Persephone
I made everything go cold
The Gods tried to tame my anger
But this time, I could not be controlled

I sent the world into darkness
Persephone, I wanted them to feel my pain
I allowed nothing to grow
And all around me, starvation reigned

Persephone, a mothers love is unmatched
And I hope this is something that you know
You are the last thing I have in this world
I'll love you wherever you go

My daughter, I know Hades loves you
He's the best God that there is
But remember that you were born wild
And Persephone, you will always be above him

Hades' Plea to Demeter

I've spent my life alone in the darkness
It is the kingdom that I rule
And my own family tossed me out
As the world labeled me cruel

Everyone knows the story
Zeus took the sky, Poseidon the sea
Then they handed me the underworld
And once again darkness welcomed me

But Persephone saw how I was shunned
She knew the stories but never ran away
Demeter, there are many times when I ask
Why the underworld is where she stays

Demeter, she is the only light I have
In a world that takes everything that I love
Let me be happy for a couple of months
Before you take her to the world above

Rhea Apologizes to Hades

Oh Hades, my sweet boy
You were always a quiet child
From the few precious moments, I had with you
I will always remember your sweet smile

I wish I could help you, my sweet boy
I know how people fear you
Hades you were always the kindest god
And I wish the world knew it too

But Persephone, sweet Aidoneus
She is a gift sent from above
Cherish her with all your heart
Because both of you deserve love

A Walk with Persephone

"Why the Underworld?" I once asked
As I walked with the Queen of the Dead
"You used to live in a world of light and color
But you traded it for death instead"

Because I was never just a minor Goddess
Her sweet silky voice replied to me
I was born with thorns under my skin
And a hunger that needed to be free

Hades loves my darkness and anger
It was him who gave me this kingdom and crown
And it is at my feet, every night
That the great King of the Underworld bows

Now instead of walking through blooming gardens
I walk on crushed petals and pomegranate seeds
The girl the world once knew is gone
And in her place rose a beautiful queen

So yes I traded daisies, tulips, and roses
I made the world lose their Goddess of spring
Because I needed to let my thorns grow
And being a queen is way more exciting

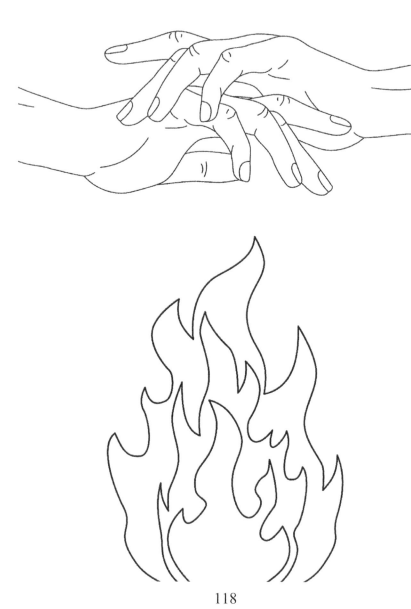

Hestia

Some say the world will end in fire
Others say it will end in ice
But I am the burning, deadly fire
And being frozen would be way more nice

The stories have forgotten me
But cities burn fires in my name
Because they know that the fire inside of me
Is impossible to tame

They say I'm the kindest Olympian
Because they haven't seen my rage
I've seen saw the destruction that fire causes
So I lock it inside a cage

I am the oldest and the youngest God
The mighty protector of the home
I am the most powerful Goddess there is
Even if I gave up my throne

Describe immortality to me in one word

The twelve Olympians sit before me, contemplating

Zeus speaks first, as a God-King should. He thinks about how he stood before his father, the youngest son, a boy lost in prophecies. He looks at his golden throne and thinks about the weight of the heavens. He has fought so hard to not be his father. Shattered glass is found in the halls of Olympus from the times when Zeus has looked in the mirror and Kronos has stared right back. He does not want to be another mad king. "Power"

Hera opens her mouth to respond. Then she closes it. She thinks about the late nights and cold beds, knowing her husband is out with a woman that is not her. She thinks about the screaming matches and spilled wine. She remembers taking her jealousy out on women like her, victims like her. She was full of anger and rage once, now she is just cold. She thinks about the girl she used to be and how trapped she is now. "Numb"

Athena speaks up next. She makes her presence known in the heavenly courtroom. She is her father's right hand, his counsel. But she fought wars for that position, angered many to become what she is today. She is wisdom, war, and woman combined and it scares everyone. She is her mother's daughter before she is her fathers. From her mother, she learned how to be cunning.

She demanded to become a War Goddess. Her grey eyes flash with unknown emotions and hidden plans. The true patron of Athens. "Battlefield"

Poseidon is not known for his peaceful waters and calm waves. He is a continuation of a legacy that was already there. He was not the beginning of the ocean. He is simply a new age, a new generation that rose from the ashes of what was already there. Poseidon is not known for being calm. At the bottom of his seas, shipwrecks line the ocean floor, a testament to his rage. "Destruction"

Apollo has only written songs about lost lovers and broken hearts since the beginning of his existence. For the God of the Sun, he does not shine as bright as he should. Caught in the rush of love, he has forgotten how the sun burns things that come too close. So many names have been carved into his heart. So many names have fallen from his lips in a cry of anguish. "Burning"

Artemis sharpens her silver arrows. She is a predator, lying in wait. When your twin is the sun, you learn very quickly that he will often overshadow you. She has become the calming afterglow to his blazing inferno. But she is not an afterthought, she carved her own destiny from the ashes of her brother. Learning when to let the wolf under her skin out and when she must keep it caged. "Eclipsing"

Demeter stopped being a soft Goddess years ago. She took the whispers that her grandmother, the Earth Goddess, gave her and she became hardened. She has found out the hard way that family means nothing to the trials of time. She refuses to become a wife like Hera, a maiden like Hestia. She is a mother before she is a Goddess. Immortality has taken everything, but it cannot take her children. "Insatiable"

Hermes has collected many titles throughout his time. He has been a guide for the dead, a thief, a messenger. He is the divine trickster and havoc in a God. Something righteous and infuriating at the same time. A silver-tongued paradox. He realized early on that being a God can weigh you down. So he became fleet-footed. He refuses to let the responsibilities of immortality pull him down like it has his family. "Consuming"

Dionysus laughs scornfully from the corner. His prolonged life had only been filled with madness and blurry days that he can't seem to remember. Immortality is not everything that it seems. He remembers being twice-born, first from his mother, then again from his father. As he looks into his wine glass, he wonders if he too should have burned as his mother did. "Illusion"

Hephaestus sits with the rest of his family in a throne room he helped design. Yet he feels isolated and different; an imposter among the perfect Gods. All of his inventions flashed through his mind. All the things he created from his scarred hands. The late nights dreaming about inventions that remain unfinished and in scraps on his workshop floor. Maybe he, too, is an unfinished masterpiece. "Flawed"

Ares has given up on being the good guy in history. He walks into his father's throne room late, bloody from his most recent war, but he doesn't care about the stains on the tiles. He meets his father's angered stare head-on, noticing how his mother refuses to meet his eyes. Ares was not always war, rage, and blood. But if you get called one thing your whole life, you start to become it. Why fight a title when you can embrace it. "Corrupting"

Aphrodite is an ancient Goddess. From the blood of Uranus, the sky, she rose. She is not a Goddess. She is love. She is love in the way that love brings life to a house. She is love when two star-crossed lovers find themselves under the night sky in each other's embrace. But Aphrodite is also love at its worst. She is love when it brings destruction and chaos. Aphrodite is love when hearts are broken in ways they cannot be repaired. "Tragic"

A Final Word from Hestia

What about you Hestia?
The oldest and youngest Olympian
The one who gave up her throne
A Goddess lost to time

What is immortality to you?

Hestia ponders the question for a moment. She prods at
the fire that she has been keeping alive for eons. Her
family will keep destroying each other until the golden
halls have become nothing but ruins. She sighs.

"Unrelenting"

Nemesis Teaches Revenge and Retribution

I am the daughter of the Night
Everyone has heard the tales
About the remorseless Nemesis
Who deals punishments with her scales

I led Narcissus to the water
Where he met a terrible end
Because his arrogance defied the Gods
So they sent the Goddess of Revenge

Don't let your hubris blind you
Mortals are not worthy of the skies
I am revenge and retribution
Angering me would be unwise

And you mortals are prideful creatures
You ask for more than what you need
So I must keep the balance
By ending those corrupted by greed

Melinoë

My parents rule the underworld
I am the saffron-cloaked Princess of the Dead
I can drive mortals like you insane
Because I know what lies in your head

I was born at the river of wailing
The princess, half-dark, half-light
I bring daunting nightmares alive
Because the shadows are my birthright

I know all of your secrets
And all of your deepest fears
I know what makes you laugh with joy
And what brings on your tears

I will turn your dreams into nightmares
And this I can guarantee
If you ever dare to test my fury
I will set your demons free

Persephone Teaches Death

Melinoë once asked her mother
"Why do good people die?
Why do the Fates cut the strings so short?
And why do they come to live with us?"

The Queen of the Underworld crouched
Brought her daughter into her arms
And allowed a single flower to grow
In the middle of her palm

"When you go into a field of flowers
Which ones do you pick?"
"The most beautiful ones"

"That is why good people die
The world cannot handle their beauty
But when they leave the living world
Their souls come to rest with us
And they live in happiness for the rest of eternity"

The Five Rivers of the Underworld

ACHERON

I sit by your shores Acheron
They call you the river of woe
Some may call you a place of healing
But that is not often how the story goes
Acheron, in you I see the pain of mortals
I see damned souls begging to be free
You are the ultimate punishment
The river of sorrow and misery

COCYTUS

Cocytus, I hear your haunting wails
They have sent shivers down my spine
Near your waters, there are lost souls
Who simply wish for more time
Like them, I cry at your solemn banks
And it is here that I will mourn
As I listen to the lamentations of the lost
My tears finally reach the shore

PHLEGETHON

In the great, fiery river of Phlegethon
Evil spirits are burned away
And when they are finally done burning
Only their very soul will remain
Phlegethon, you are the river of the wicked
It is into Tartarus that you flow
Along your banks, evil spirits drink your fire
From your forever blazing inferno

LETHE

Take my pain and my sorrow
In your forgetful waters, I shall fall
Lethe, take my memories and my life
For you can have it all
Take this special piece of me
Lethe, allow me to forget
I wish to start all over again
And this time, I want no regrets

STYX

I swear an oath upon the river Styx
One that even Gods would not dare to break
Everyone knows how you deal with curse breakers
And the destruction that lies in your wake
It will be at your darkened waters
Where destiny and I will have our last rendezvous
In the end, my life will be yours
Styx, this oath I swear to you

A Message from Nike

You, my little warrior
I know how tired you are
But never stop fighting
Trust me, your victory is not far

You are victory personified
This is a war that you will win
Because I have seen your heart
And the fire that rages within

They want you to break
But they could never defeat you
You are golden winged victory
And the world should know it too

You are blessed by the victorious Nike
And you will burn brighter than the sun
Go rest your weary head, my warrior
Because your battle is finally done

Iris

If I gave you a paintbrush Iris
Would you paint rainbows in the sky?
Would you learn to create new colors
That leave others memorized?

You tried to pick a favorite color
But then you decided to use them all
Now your masterpieces dance across the world
Leaving everyone enthralled

The Nine Muses

Sing to me, harmonious Calliope
Tell me of heroes, monsters, and men
And once you've told me of Perseus and Heracles
Tell me all the stories again

Whisper to me, ancient Clio
The sweet proclaimer of history
Tell me about mighty nations forming
And the rise and fall of kings

Mourn with me, devastating Melpomene
The singer of great tragedy
I hear your songs of misfortune
And the riveting aches in your melodies

Give me a tune, lyrical Euterpe
Sweet muse, the giver of delight
Let emotional rhymes fall from your lips
As your beautiful prose fills the silent night

Award me love, desired Erato
Write about how love fills the air
Tell me how love can heal the deepest wounds
But also cause the most despair

Dance with me, light-footed Terpsichore
I can see the magic as you spin
Reveal all your stories as you move
And show the emotions you hold within

Gaze with me, heavenly Urania
Let us watch as the stars fill the Skies
Point out different celestial bodies to me
As universes are born before our eyes

Laugh with me, joyous Thalia
Tell me jokes to make me smile
With you, I laugh freely and loudly
Something I haven't done in a while

Quiet me, wise Polyhymnia
So I may hear what you are to say
You are the one of many hymns
And I will try to win your praise

Eros' Wrath

Eros shot Apollo full of love
Then he shot Daphne full of hate
Deep down, he knew how this story would end
But it was a risk he was willing to take

Apollo tempted Eros' wrath
Tried to make him look like a fool
But Apollo forgot about love
And how often it is cruel

Daphne

Being loved by a God is scary
Especially if you don't love him in return
When the God of the Sun loves you
You will both end up getting burned

Apollo never stopped chasing me
All I could ever do was run
The day soon became my enemy
As I began to resent the sun

Eventually, I became too tired
I couldn't bare to run anymore
So I cried to my father for help
And freedom was all I could pray for

Being loved by a God is scary
It often feels like a curse
So I became the famed laurel tree
Because being loved seemed so much worse

Remembering Nymphs

I pray to
Daphne,
Acantha,
Maia,
Callisto,
Thetis,
Io,
and countless others

So often are nymphs damned by Gods
So often are nymphs, victims of jealousy
So often are nymphs caught in godly affairs

I pray to all of you
Provide me with the strength to survive
In a world designed to consume you

Eris Learns Chaos

I learned chaos from my grandmother
When my mother was busy
Dragging her darkness across the sky
My grandmother would sit with me
As we gazed out at the galaxies that she created
With her own two hands
She told me something
"My blood runs through your veins
Thousands of stars are exploding under your skin
You are calamity and discord
I may be the chaos that built this universe
But you, my dear
You will be the chaos that destroys it"

141

Eris' Revenge

You can have my golden apple
If you're the fairest one of all
And you Goddesses don't see it now
But this will be your downfall

They denied me an invitation
Goddess of Chaos, daughter of Nyx
So I promised them revenge
And I swore it on the river Styx

They forgot about my love of war
How I look at bloodshed with glee
They should know what happens
When you let discord run free

They made a mistake forgetting me
I started the Trojan War just for fun
They wanted to tame my chaos
But I answer to no one

IV. The Mortal Age

"There is beauty in mortality
When you cherish every moment
Live in every moment
Breathe in every moment
That is how you know
You are truly alive"

Cry Helen

they will sing of beautiful Helen
who launched a thousand ships
and brought the end of Troy
on pretty painted lips

Helen of No One

My whole life I was treated as property
My father sold me away
But I held my temper behind a dazzling facade
Because I knew I would make them all pay

Menelaus, you made me Queen of Sparta
You did not see the promise of death in my smile
You wanted to claim the beautiful Helen
But you will never tame something so wild

And Paris, you stole me away
Like an alluring prize, you got to keep
But every night I sang for the end of Troy
While you were beside me, fast asleep

You all forget, my true father is the King of the Heavens
Golden Ichor runs through my veins
I am Helen of No One but myself
And you cannot keep a Goddess chained

The Arsonist

My beauty craved fire
Menelaus, I was too raw for you
I was a kingdom destroyer
I have always been a queen
Paris, you were blind
I wanted the end of Troy
I needed your city to fall
I saw Troy alight with fire
And as it burned before my eyes
All I could do was smile

The Wrath of Achilles

When you died, my rage shook the earth
They could not tame my wrath
I cut down Trojan warriors
As my sorrow became a bloodbath

Patroclus, I was almost a God
Every inch of me but my heel
And the pain I felt after losing you
Made death a much sweeter ordeal

Patroclus, why did you leave me
You're the only thing that kept me alive
You, my silly, foolish boy
Why did you have to die?

And you stupid, naive creature
I have only one question for you
Why join a battle you couldn't win
If our story was not through?

Questioning Apollo

Why did you guide that arrow?
The one the ended Achilles
What did you have
Against the fallen hero?

Because I have known the pain
Of losing lovers to the Fates' games
And in that moment
I would rather be with them in death
Than alone in life
I did not get the choice
But he did

Cassandra

Cursed, ill-fated Cassandra
Who spills prophecies from her tongue
You saw the catastrophic end of Troy
But you were believed by no one

Tragic, priestess Cassandra
The future has always haunted you
The whispers of destruction and death
And only you knew they were true

Haunted, lonely Cassandra
You knew Helen had a destructive plan
But why would they listen to you?
What made you wiser than a man?

Solemn, fruitless Cassandra
You tried but it was in vain
And I hope people only offer apologies
Whenever they dare speak your name

Remembering Penelope

They will sing songs of beautiful Helen
Of Cassandra and her cursed tongue
But they will forget you, dear Penelope
And the battles that you have won

Odysseus left you to defend Ithaca
He forced you to become king that day
And it was with your cunning mind
That you kept your suitors at bay

Maybe you didn't set a thousand ships a sail
Or spell out foreshadowing prophecies
But you are a wise, powerful woman
And you display it flawlessly

Calypso's Tragedy

The Gods are selfish beings
They've been since the beginning of time
I fell in love with you, Odysseus
And to the Gods that was a crime

As if my heart didn't break
Every time I heard you cry her name
You sang for home and sweet Penelope
And looked at me with disdain

I had no choice but to love you
Even though you'd leave me here alone
I fell in love with you willingly
Because loneliness was all I had ever known

In the end, you left me, Odysseus
Because the Gods are selfish things
Goddesses cannot love mortal men
And you will only ever love Penelope

Dear Danaë

They hail Perseus for his journey
But speak nothing of your sacrifice
You are the mother of a hero
And for him, you almost lost your life

Your own father hid you away
Because of a prophecy, you did not choose
You became an object of affection
Loved by Polydectes and Zeus

You are a survivor Danaë
You have been through so many things
You took your destiny and made it yours
Now you're a woman that terrifies kings

Andromeda

They chained you, naked, to a rock
And turned you into a sacrifice
Your mother acted against the Gods
But it was you who paid the price

The stories read that Perseus saved you
As if you'd ever rely on a man again
Your own father gave you up for his kingdom
So you took your fate into your hands

You became a supernova
The bright, powerful explosion of a star
It's not your face that makes you beautiful
It's the way the sky dances with your scars

You are not a sacrifice, a prize, a consort
You are constellations and galaxies
How dare they try to belittle you?
When cosmos are born as you breathe

156

Persephone and Orpheus

I mourn for your loss Orpheus
Death is cruelest to the living
But now I must warn you to be careful
Because Death is not forgiving

You will want to look at her
Sometimes your temptation will be too great
But Orpheus you have been given a second chance
Do not lose her to the hands of fate

I mourn the plight of lovers
This world is not often kind
Keep walking forward young poet
Trust that she will always be behind

A Goodbye From Eurydice

Sing a tune for me lyrical Orpheus
Let this be our last goodbye
I will see you again one day
But for now, sing to me one last time

Ariadne to Theseus

My half-brother was born a monster
And there is a little monster in me
So I guess that's why you left me, Theseus
Because I am demanded to be free

I was never born to love you
Or be the prize at your journey's end
I am not a token or a trophy
I won't be the princess you get to win

In many ways, I am a puzzle
The labyrinth that you could never solve
You tried to use strings to control me
But I am not your puppet doll

I had too much darkness for you
You thought I was broken and flawed
But Dionysus loves every part of me
Why have a hero when you can have a God

Ariadne's Love

You gave up a hero for a God
You knew that Theseus was too good
Too gentle
Too heroic
For you to truly fall in love with him
You were charmed by him at first
You saw him as a ticket
A way to get out of the maze
That was your own life
And when he abandoned you
You danced in joy so beautifully
So freely
So wonderfully
That the God of Wine
Fell in love with you
His madness matched your own
And together, you healed each other

Eros and Psyche

When Aphrodite promised me to a monster
I wept every day in despair
But Eros couldn't hurt me
He knew that Gods were rarely fair

He asked that I wouldn't look upon him
That's the only thing he wanted from me
But I gazed at his godly beauty once
And he flew away, far and free

But I loved Eros with everything
He gave me a second chance at life
So I completed Aphrodite's tasks
Because he was worth the strife

And when he came back to me
Like an angel sent from above
I asked to become a Goddess
And spend eternity with the God of Love

Aphrodite tells Eros of Love

I learned love from my mother
But she could only tell me of heartache
She told me the dangers of falling in love
Of crashing to the ground
And breaking into a million pieces
Hoping the one you fell for
Would pick you up
And glue you back together
But sometimes they will not be there
And not repair what they broke
However, on special nights
My mother would tell me of soulmates
Of the epic love stories that
Bring nations together
The type of love
That wars are fought over
Those were my favorite stories
The love stories that build things
Not destroy them

The Fate of Hyacinth

it was a beautiful day

you and your Hyacinth were in a field
the grass swayed with the soft wind
as it graced the two lovers
lost in each other's presence.
you had forgotten what it meant to be a God.
you began to feel mortal.
for the first time in ages, you felt alive
full of purpose.
you looked at your beautiful Hyacinth
who was caught in a moment of joy
and as he smiled at you
he had never looked so ethereal
then the soft wind that was once there
turned cold
as Zephyrs jealousy raged
you suddenly remembered the maliciousness of Gods
you remembered that Gods are not forgiving
and you watched him fall
your Hyacinth
if your heart could stop
it would have
you tried to cry out to him
but the voice that once sang love songs
just would not come out

164

the once green grass became red
and then flowers sprouted around his fallen body
like Persephone herself
allowed for there to be beauty in his death
you learned then what Helios meant
when he told you that being the God of the Sun
is the loneliest path there is

The Sun's Pain

With a broken chuckle, Apollo cried
Icarus' fallen form in his arms
"You silly boy" he whispered
"You're just like all the others,
Trying to love the sun
Who will always only bring pain to those
Who try to touch its beauty"

The Golden Boy

In the stories, I'm a foolish boy
Who got drunk on the feeling of being free
And ignored his father's warnings
As he fell like a stone to the sea

I knew what I wanted all along
And when my father gave me a chance to fly
I let my wings use the seas salty breeze
So I could reach the sun that hung so high

I had always known of the dangers
But I was only drunk on the idea of love
I knew the fate of mortals in love with Gods
And yet, I still wanted a taste of the sun

So with golden wings, I took off
Giving the land below a grand farewell
And once I gave the sun my fiery kiss
I laughed loudly as I fell

Asking Icarus

I once asked Icarus
Why he loved the sun so much
That he would risk his own life
For a single, burning touch

And he replied to me
With burnt wings and stormy eyes
I'd risk my whole life again,
Just for the chance to kiss the sunrise

A Father's Fallen Angel

I knew he was a fallen angel
Who would crave to return to the sun
I had hoped I could hold him longer
But the sun grants wishes to no one

I knew he heard the sirens call
I saw how he looked at the sea below
One day, the ocean would take him away
And I would have to let him go

Hyacinth and Icarus Talk of Love

I loved the sun

As did I

What fools we were
To fall in love with a God
Even though we knew the warnings
Even though we knew the pain
Even though we saw the dangers
That awaited us

Yes, it was foolish
But I will never regret it
I never felt as free as
When I tried to fly into the suns grasp
And started to fall
But the fall was not bad
It was like falling in love with the sun
All over again

…
I would do it again too
Mortals and Gods shouldn't mix
But when they do it is beautiful
And he was beautiful
Then, when I died

I became something beautiful
I will always love the sun
Even if it cost me everything

I will always love him too
For the is the plight of dreamers
In love with the sun

Echo

The Queen of the Gods cursed me
Now I'm forever a second thought
And Aphrodite did not warn me
About the pain that love brought

I was forced into the shadows
Where no one ever heard my words
For that was the curse of Echo
Never seen and never heard

Trust me, I know the trials of love
I once fell, but it was all in vain
Narcissus could never see the real me
Instead of love, he brought me pain

You must never fade into the background
Please take some advice from me
Do not waste your love on boys like him
Boys who crush you and take everything

The Fate of Adonis

Adonis, you were a beautiful boy
Some called you an angel from above
But you fell into a dangerous trap
And got entangled with the Goddess of Love

It is said that she truly loved you
The Gods saw how she held you when you died
And her scream of anguish were so heartbreaking
That the whole world flinched as she cried

Zeus and Styx

Zeus stared down
At the wide-eyed innocent Semele
Who had asked him to reveal
His full glory before her

He hesitated

But Styx stood behind him
An everlasting reminder
"Can I save this one?"
He whispered to Styx

You swore an oath on my name.
Styx replied grimly
**You'd be a fool to break it
over a mortal girl**

A tear also burned in the presence of his true form

Zeus' Apology to Semele

I wish you listened, my Semele
But there was nothing I could do
Gods simply burn too bright
For mortals such as you

You were one of the special ones
But I was selfish to fall in love
There were so many warnings
That I did not warn you of

I may have failed you Semele
But I will protect our son
I have lost so many people
And he will not be another one

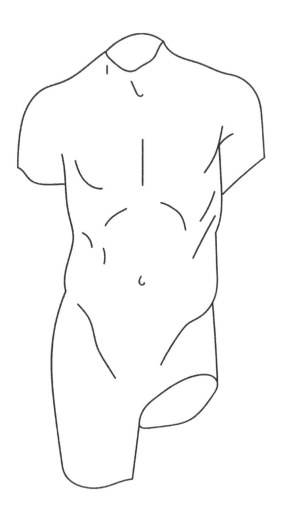

178

Heracles Mourns Megara

When you become a hero
The people around you become victims
And if a hero lives long enough
You will start to lose your humanity
Pieces of you begin to chip away
Because of the things you have seen

Megara you were my wife
And in madness, I killed you
Now I am both monster and hero
A true, divine paradox
Who should I blame for my misfortune?

Should I blame the Goddess?
The one who has hated me from birth?
Should I blame my father?
For he knows what happens to his sons
Who become heroes

Should I blame myself?
I should have known the dangers
Loving a hero is fatal
And I should have warned you Megara
You can die a hero
Or live long enough to become a monster

The Tragedy of Iphigenia

I remember betrayal
I remember my father's hands
Leading me down the aisle
His eyes, filled with tears
But not with the joyful sorrow
A father should have
Handing away his daughter
On her wedding day
No, he knew what awaited me
I was walking to my death with a smile
Until I realized what was happening
This was an execution
I looked at my father
Eyeing the golden knife
Gripped in his clenched hands
And I smiled sadly
For I had always been a daddy's girl
I said to him
Look me in the eye when you do it
When you kill me.
Do not become a coward now
He hesitated
Before swiping the steel blade
Clean across my neck
I don't remember much
But I remember gold dissolving around me

My father's tear stricken face
And the moon
I remember the moon
Along with the soft whisper of Artemis
You are just a child
Not a bargaining chip

Arachne's Hubris

I should have known better
I tempted a Goddess' wrath
But pride is a dangerous addiction
And I had already paved my path

I wanted to be legendary
I wanted people to remember my name
So I challenged the Goddess Athena
For just a brief taste of fame

I made a beautiful tapestry
Not even Athena herself could lie
I depicted broken, deceitful Gods
And I had forgotten that Gods are not kind

The Wisdom Goddess cursed me
So my warning is to be careful with your pride
You can never be better than the Gods
And you shouldn't even try

The Savior Pandora

Pandora, sweet hero girl
The one who saved us all
The Gods thought that her gift of curiosity
Would be our fatal downfall

Disease, poverty, misery, sadness, and death
The things released from Pandora's box
But despite all the darkness released
She gave us something worth the costs

Pandora gave us Hope
And Hope is a beautiful thing
It heals the hearts that have been hurt
By the destruction that evil brings

Pandora gave us a reason to live
For there is beauty in sickness and death
It makes us realize the importance of life
And makes us cherish every breath

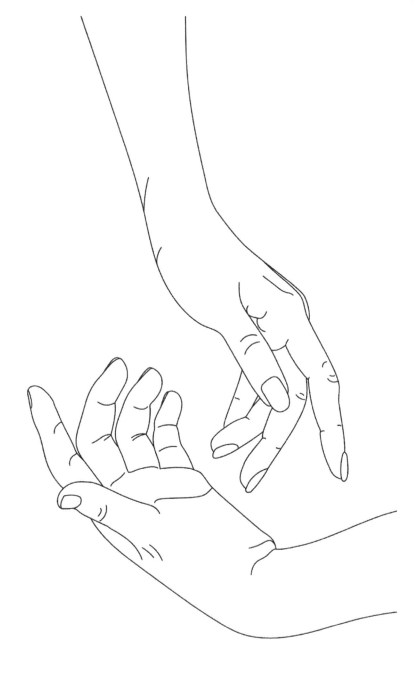

Pandora of molded clay
You defied the Gods
And released Hope amongst all evils

Thank You

Artemis to Atalanta

You were born wild Atalanta
Born to run faster than the wind
You have fought battles fearlessly
And I can see it on your skin

I am giving you this warning
Be wary of the hearts of men
Their hearts, full of greed and lust
Always hate to see women win

There is nothing more powerful than you
A woman, confident in herself
You have a warriors heart within
I look at you and see myself

Oh Meleager

You may love Atalanta
But that will never be enough
She will always protect herself first
Even if that means giving you up

You have seen her in battle
Covered in blood, soaked to the bone
You saw how she cut down enemies
With one single, deadly blow

Your love will not protect you
This is not a sport, not a game
I would hate to see what happens
If you try to keep her tamed

You will never own her Meleager
Like the earth, she is wild
Even the greatest of kings shiver
When she flashes her lethal smile

Hippolyta

She was born with the blood of the War God
Golden Ichor runs through her veins
She is the queen of the mighty Amazons
In battle, they cry her name

She earned her right to be queen
Her name has become notorious
She enters battle with a glint in her eyes
And leaves the field victorious

She is a Goddess trapped by mortality
Her ferocity has never been seen
She is both warrior and woman
And what a dangerous thing to be

The Birth of Amazons

I. we were wolves before we were women.

II. our fur gave way to skin and we rose with an insatiable hunger yearning to be set free.

III. The Gods began to fear us, a race of warrior women, who sharpened their teeth into canines, who remember that being complacent was never their cup of tea, who remember the moon.

IV. we were wolves before we were women.

190

Chained Prometheus

"Was it worth it?" I asked
As I looked upon the chained Prometheus
The forgotten, punished Titan
"Mortals have taken your gift
Your life
Your fire
And we have turned it into war
Into pain
Into death
When the vulture arrives every day
Does it whisper in your ear?
And tell you how humans destroy themselves?
Does it hurt you
Knowing that your beautiful clay creations
Are they ruining themselves?
Do you cry for them?"
I look at the chained Prometheus
As a tear slides down his aged face
"Was it worth it?
Being punished for those
Who never appreciated your sacrifice?"

Mortality

There is a special beauty in death
Every day you live is a gift to you
Life becomes more remarkable
When from your first breath you are doomed

And no one will ever tell you this
The Gods and their stubborn pride
But they envy mortals like us
Because we are actually alive

There is nothing beautiful in immortality
When you don't need to count every breath
But being mortal means each day could be your last
That is why there is beauty in death

V. The Monster Age

Am I a monster?
"No.
You are human
You are a human who has been hurt
And to save yourself
You became dangerous
You are not a monster."

Echidna and Typhon

Typhon, you did not make me into a monster
I was a monster before you
You loved the darkest pieces of myself
And I loved your pieces too

You are genuinely something wicked
The deadliest creature ever known
And you will bring the end of kingdoms
Causing kings to be dethroned

I am monster and girl combined
Half Goddess, half hell
They call me "The Goddess fierce Echidna"
And I wear that title well

I am the mother of many monsters
You are the Gods greatest nightmare
And when we are together
Even the mighty Zeus gets scared

The Tale of Medusa

I was once a naive girl
Till I learned to hate the sea
It took all the innocence I had
And ripped it away from me

That is where she found me
Broken and bruised on her temple floor
So she offered me revenge against men
The wise Goddess of War

Now they say male heroes fear me
Even Gods don't look in my eyes
They say one gaze from me
Will bring about a swift demise

And maybe you can't hurt male Gods
Cannot make them bleed
But I've seen women turn into monsters
And that's all the power they need

Athena cursed you
And you still call her your Goddess?

Oh the wisdom Goddess never cursed me
Athena took my soft eyes, my hair,
She took my vulnerable skin
That had been ruined by men
And she made me feral
Something that men will always fear
So that I would be an example
Of what happens when a man breaks an innocent girl
And a monster rises in her place

Medusa Speaks (Medusa to Perseus)

I am sure you've heard the tales, young hero
But they have filled your head with lies
No one has ever told you my story
Or why I curse those who look in my eyes

I am the victim in this tale
The God of the Oceans came to me
One night, he took everything I held dear
And left me broken on my knees

I prayed to the wise Athena for help
I wanted vengeance that she couldn't give
I knew that Gods were never held accountable
But this was something I could never forgive

So Athena made me into something dangerous
She made venom from my fallen tears
My eyes that had once enchanted gods
Soon became something that all men feared

I became the infamous monster gladly
I wanted to be a warning to all men
My rage soon became a weapon
As I hid death within my grin

Maybe you will end me, young hero
But at least I told you my tale
I am not the villain they told you I was
I am just a girl who traded skin for scales

200

The Enchantress

Men have called you an enchantress
They've stripped the title of Goddess from you
Your name was slandered in history
But your redemption is long overdue

They wanted you to appear weak
To them, your strength was a sin
But relish in the fear they hold, Circe
Make them fear the magic within

Men tremble at the mention of your name
For they've heard of your poisoned wine
The tales of Odysseus and his men
And how you turned them into swine

The stories have made you into a villain
But this is the reckoning hour
You are a true Goddess, Circe
And they will all burn in your power

Siren

Let me sing to you, wise sailor
A song of promise and lust
Please follow the sound of my voice
Because in me, you must trust

I am everything you have ever wanted
Sailor, come and join me
Listen to my beautiful song
As you swim across the sea

I am not a little mermaid
I am death and broken dreams
To you, sailor, I am a mythical beauty
But beauty is not always what it seems

Sailor, men like you are so foolish
Darling, you noticed the danger too late
And you will see my true form
Right before I crush you against the waves

Scylla

You were more than a monster once
A poor naiad trapped in godly affairs
You didn't want to be loved by the sea God
But the Fates rarely answer prayers

Poseidon tried to protect you
Tried to shield you from his wife's jealousy
Without warning, he turned you into a monster
And you flung yourself into the sea

You wandered the sea for ages
Then you made yourself home on rocky cliffs
Now you prey on wandering men
Sailing by on unsuspecting ships

You may have been a helpless naiad once
Now you have become something stronger
But as you crash ships on your rocks, remember
You were once more than a monster

Becoming Charybdis

She is a woman conquering
Bringing destruction with her waves
She slowly consumes every piece of you
As she drags you to a watery grave

She is a maelstrom waiting
A monster chained to the seafloor
She begins to draw you in slowly
Until you lose sight of the sandy shore

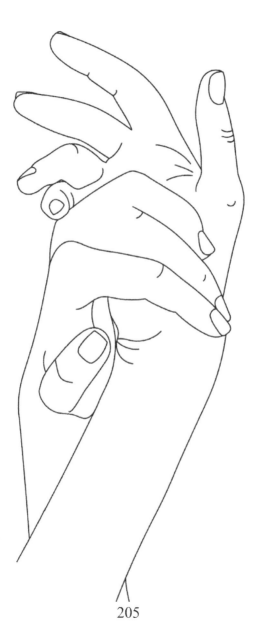

205

Women Becoming Monsters

Bless me Medusa
Give me your scales and frightful eyes
Give me the power that lurks under your skin
Turn me into something weaponized

Bless me Charybdis
Let my emotions become the tides
So that I can drown my enemies
With the storm, I hold inside

Bless me Circe
Carve your spells into my hips
Teach me how to become an enchantress
Allow Latin to spill from my lips

Bless me Sirens
Sing to me your enchanting songs
I will lure men into my grasp
Before they realize something is wrong

Bless me Scylla
Turn me into a sailor's nightmare
Make me into something so frightening
That even the mightiest of heroes get scared

VI. The Final Age

"The Bright Age of the Gods is gone
But it lives on through you
Share this history with the world"

The Gods are gone.
Modernity and technology have paved over
The ancient temples of Gods
Like Zeus and Poseidon
And their feats have become myths
Stories told in English classes
The Gods are gone.

You now stand before Atlas
Who still holds the world
On his broken, bloody knees

"The Gods are gone."
You whisper
"So why do you continue to hold the world?
Why do you continue to punish yourself?"

"If I don't hold the world
No one will"

You reach out with open arms

"Let me help."

You are a Goddess

You carry ancient magic in your veins
Chaos carved you from her cosmos
And Gaea then breathed life in you
You are a Goddess

In your heart, Hestia's fire burns
You learned to fight from Artemis
And Athena blessed you with wisdom

While Demeter taught you how to nurture the earth
Every part of you was cherished by Aphrodite
And when you are angry
I pray for everyone

For you carry Hera's rage in your veins

A Divine Legacy

Do not name your daughters after Goddesses
Or Queens
Or warriors

Allow her to carve her own path
Make her way into history books on her own
Not as someone who was already there
But as her own person

Give her a rare name
So that she knows from birth
That she is something remarkable
She will learn to be confident in herself

And when her name is called
The entire world will pause
Waiting to hear her speak
And heed her command

Generations of Goddesses

What is it like giving birth to a Goddess?

Ask my mother
And my grandmother
And my great grandmother

Trace my family line back generations
Slowly our blood became gold
And Goddesses were born instead of women

We learned to mix ambrosia with our food
Learned how to keep our power at bay
When men began to call us witches

At night, we chased the stars we put in the sky
We drank and we sang and we laughed
As we let chaos and Latin run through our veins

We have always been Goddesses
We have been Goddesses for generations
Pulling the strings of the world around us

Girls Becoming Goddesses

It starts when you are young.
Your parents gifted you barbies, makeup, and princess dresses.
When deep down you wanted to be a pirate, with plastic swords instead of tiaras.
You then decided to become the best pirate princess the world had ever seen.

On the playgrounds at school, the boys wouldn't play with you because you're "too girly" and "too weak".
And the girls said you were simply "too tough" to play with them.
So you become rouge and start to find friends in the shadows that tell you, *you were born golden.*

As you grow up, society starts to take your childhood wishes and give you responsibilities too young.
They begin to dictate what you can wear, what you can do, and when you can speak.
But you have never been one for being quiet and you demanded the world to hear your voice.

Being an adult has its own set of challenges and expectations of you.
You will have to work twice as hard to get the same pay as a man and those you work with will forget how much you are worth.

So become your own boss and make twice as much money.

You will change from girl to Goddess quietly
A silent metamorphosis
When you realize that the sky has always spoken to you.
When you realize that you were stronger than anyone who has ever hurt you.
When you realize that being yourself is the strongest weapon that you own.

You were born golden.

GLOSSARY

Acheron: One of the Five Rivers of the Underworld. River of Woe.

Achilles: Greek hero warrior in the Trojan War. As an infant, his mother, Thetis (a sea nymph) dipped him in the River Styx, holding him by his heel, his only vulnerable part. The lover of Patroclus.

Adonis: A lover of Aphrodite who died when Ares (or Artemis) sent a wild boar after him.

Aether: The Primordial personification of the light. The son of Nyx (Night) and Erebus (Darkness) and the sister of Hemera (Day).

Agamemnon: The King of Mycenae, brother of Menelaus and the father of Iphigenia. Commanded the Greek forces in the Trojan War.

the Amazons: A race of warrior women who descended from Ares. The Queen of the Amazons is Hippolyta.

Amphitrite: The Sea Goddess and the Queen of the Seas; wife of Poseidon. She is a Nereid, a daughter of Nereus and Doris.

Andromeda: The Princess of Aethiopia, daughter of King Cepheus and Queen Cassiopeia. When Cassiopeia bragged about Andromeda's beauty, she upset Poseidon who demanded that Andromeda be chained to a rock as a sacrifice. She was saved by the hero, Perseus.

Aphrodite: The Goddess of Love and Beauty. She was formed from Uranus' castration and seafoam. One of the Twelve Olympian Gods.

Apollo: The God of the Sun, Healing, and Poetry. Son of Zeus and Leto, twin brother of Artemis. He got the gift of prophecy from his grandmother, the Titanide Phoebe. One of the Twelve Olympians.

Arachne: A victim of hubris, Arachne challenged Athena to a weaving contest. When Arachne portrayed the Gods with flaws, Athena cursed the girl and Arachne became the first spider.

Ares: The God of War. Son of Zeus and Hera. One of the Twelve Olympians. Lover of Aphrodite.

Ariadne: The Princess of Crete, daughter of King Minos and Queen Pasiphaë, half-sister of the minotaur. She helped Theseus escape the labyrinth and left Crete with him. Later, Theseus abandoned her on the shores of Naox where Dionysus found and married her.

Artemis: The Goddess of the Hunt, the Moon, and the Wild. She is the daughter of Zeus and Leto and the twin sister of Apollo. Granddaughter of Phoebe. One of the Twelve Olympians.

Asteria: The Titan Goddess of Falling Stars and Nighttime Divination. She ran from Zeus' advances, transforming into an island. Mother of Hecate.

Atalanta: The swift-footed virgin huntress who was unwilling to marry and loved by the hero Meleager.

Athena: The Goddess of Wisdom and War. She is the daughter of Zeus and Metis. One of the Twelve Olympians.

Atlas: A Titan who was one of the leaders of the Titans in the Titanomachy. Condemned by Zeus to hold the sky as a punishment.

Atropos: One of the Three Fates or Moirai. Cuts the threads of life.

Calypso: Daughter of Atlas, forced to live alone on the island of Ogygia. Fell in love with Odysseus, but her advances were scorned.

Cassandra: The Princess of Troy. Daughter of King Priam and Queen Hecuba. After she rejected Apollo's advances, she was cursed to speak prophecies that no one would believe.

Chaos (Khaos): The first Primordial God. The personification of the chasm from which all Primordial Gods come from and the creator of everything in Greek Myths.

Charybdis: A sea monster who was chained to the seafloor by Zeus, where she forms a whirlpool of water that sucks in ships and sailors. Scylla and her make a dangerous strait in the Messina.

Circe: The Goddess of Sorcery who lived on the island Aeaea. The daughter of Helios. She turned men to pigs with wine.

Clotho: One of the Three Fates or Moirai. She spins the threads of human life.

Cocytus: One of the Five Rivers of the Underworld. River of Wailing.

the Cyclopes: Children of Uranus (Sky) and Gaea (Earth). They were thrown into Tartarus with their brothers, the Hecatoncheires by their father for how they looked.

Danaë: Mother of Perseus. She was impregnated by Zeus when he came to her locked chamber in the form of a golden shower. Her father threw both her and the baby into the sea in a locked box in fear. She then caught the attention of Polydectes but rejected him.

Daphne: A Naiad who ran from Apollo's advances after Eros shot her with a leaden hate arrow and Apollo with a golden love arrow. Eventually, she cried to her father to transform her into the laurel tree.

Demeter: The Goddess of Harvest, Fertility, and Agriculture. Daughter of Kronos and Rhea. Mother of Persephone (Kore). One of the Twelve Olympians.

Dionysus: The God of Wine, Madness, and Religious Ecstasy. Son of Zeus and Semele. Husband of Ariadne. He was twice-born, once by his mother before she was killed, and then by Zeus, who placed the baby in his thigh. One of the Twelve Olympians.

Echidna: The Mother of Monsters. Half woman, half-snake. The mate of the fearsome monster, Typhon.

Echo: A nymph cursed by Hera to only repeat the last words said. She fell in love with Narcissus, who was cursed by Nemesis to fall in love with his reflection. Echo watched him fall in love with himself.

Erebus: The Primordial personification of Darkness. A child of Chaos. The husband of Nyx (Night).

Eris: The Goddess of Discord. After she was not invited to the wedding of Thetis and Peleus, she threw a golden apple into the wedding titled "The Fairest Goddess of All". This started an argument between Hera, Aphrodite, and Athena. Eris inadvertently started the Trojan War.

Eros: The God of Love and Passion. Husband of Psyche

Eurydice: The wife of Orpheus, who died from a snake bite. Orpheus loved her so dearly that he tried to rescue her from the Underworld, but looked back at her and failed.

Eurynome: A pre-Olympian Queen who was overthrown by Rhea and Kronos.

Gaea: The Primordial Personification of the Earth. The first child of Chaos. Married to Uranus.

the Gorgons: Three powerful monsters, Medusa, Stehno, and Euryale. They are mostly known for the only mortal sister, Medusa.

Hades: The God of the Dead and Hidden Wealth, King of the Underworld. Eldest son of Kronos and Rhea.

Hecate (Hekate): The Goddess of Necromancy. Daughter of Asteria. Resides in the Underworld.

the Hecatoncheires: The Hundred Handed Giants were three sons of Gaea (Earth) and Uranus (sky). They were cast into Tartarus with their brothers, the Cyclopes.

Helen: The Queen of Sparta and the wife of King Menelaus. Daughter of Zeus and Leda. She ran away with Paris, the Prince of Troy. She is known as "the face that launched a thousand ships"

Helios: The God of the Sun. Son of Hyperion and brother of Selene and Eos.

Hemera: The Primordial personification of the Day. Daughter of Nyx (Night) and Erebus (Darkness).

Hephaestus: The God of Blacksmiths, Forges, and Metalworking. Son of Zeus and Hera. When he was born, Hera tossed him off Olympus. One of the Twelve Olympians. Husband of Aphrodite.

Hera: The Goddess of Marriage and Childbirth and the Queen of Olympus. Daughter of Kronos and Rhea. Wife of Zeus. One of the Twelve Olympians.

Heracles: Grecian Hero. Son of Zeus and Alcmene. Driven mad by Hera, he kills his wife, Megara, and their children. He is given twelve labors to redeem himself.

Hermes: The God of Thieves, Trickery, and Boundaries. Son of Zeus and Maia. He is the messenger of the Olympians. One of the Olympian Gods.

Hestia: The Virgin Goddess of the Hearth, the Home, and Family. The eldest child of Kronos and Rhea. She was one of the Twelve Olympians but she gave up her throne. It was filled with Dionysus.

Hippolyta: The Queen of the Amazons and the daughter of Ares.

Hyacinth: A hero and lover of Apollo. He was killed by a flying discus. Around his fallen form, the Hyacinth flower sprouted.

Icarus: The son of Daedalus, creator of the labyrinth. Icarus and Daedalus were imprisoned by Minos on an island. To escape, Daedalus crafted wings of feathers and wax. Daedalus warned Icarus not to fly too close to the sun or the sea, but Icarus ignored his warnings and flew too high, where his wings burned and he fell towards the sea.

Iphigenia: Daughter of Agamemnon who was sacrificed by her father so the Greek troops could sail to Troy. In some versions, the Goddess Artemis sees her courage and saves her.

Iris: The Goddess of Rainbows and the Messenger of the Gods.

Kronos: The King of the Titans and the father of the Olympians. He was king before he was dethroned by Zeus.

Lachesis: One of the Three Fates or Moirai. She measures the threads of destiny.

Lethe: One of the Five Rivers of the Underworld. River of Forgetfulness.

Leto: The Titan Goddess of Motherhood. Sister of Asteria and the mother of Artemis and Apollo.

Medusa: She was originally a high priestess at Athena's temple where she became a victim of Poseidon's lust. She then prayed to Athena for help, who turned her into a monster with snakes for hair and the ability to turn anyone who looked her in the eye, into stone.

Megara: The wife of Heracles. She was murdered along with her children by Heracles in a fit of madness.

Melinoë: The Goddess of Nightmares and Madness. The daughter of Persephone.

Menelaus: The King of Sparta and the husband of Helen of Troy. The brother of Agamemnon.

Metis: The Goddess of Cunning. She was the first wife of Zeus before he devoured her because it was prophesied that their first son would overthrow him. Mother of Athena.

Mnemosyne: The Titan Goddess of Memory and one of the Twelve Original Titans. Mother of the Nine Muses.

Nemesis: The Goddess of Revenge and Retribution.
Nike: The Goddess of Personified Victory.

Nyx: The Primordial personification of the Night. Daughter of Chaos and the mother of many Gods and Goddesses.

Odysseus: The King of Itacha who journeyed for ten years after he left Ithaca to fight in the Trojan War. Husband of Penelope. Favored by Athena for his cunning.

Orpheus: A musician, poet, and prophet. The son of Apollo. Ventured to the Underworld to retrieve his wife, Eurydice, but failed.

Pandora: The first mortal woman molded from clay by Hephaestus. She was given a box that contained all the evils in the world, which she released along with Hope.

Paris: The Prince of Troy who ran away with Helen, the Queen of Sparta. He played a part in starting the Trojan War after he chose Aphrodite over Athena and Hera, when asked to give the apple of discord to the Goddess he found most beautiful, angering the others.

Patroclus: The lover of Achilles and warrior in the Trojan War. When he was killed, Achilles single-handedly destroyed most of the Trojan troops.

Penelope: The Queen of Ithaca and wife of Odysseus. She used her knowledge to keep the suitors that threatened to marry her at bay while her husband was gone.

Persephone: The Goddess of Spring and the Queen of the Underworld. Daughter of Demeter, wife of Hades, mother to Melinoë.

Perseus: A Grecian Hero. Son of Zeus and Danaë. He slew Medusa and later married Andromeda.

Phlegethon: One of the Five Rivers of the Underworld. River of Fire.

Phoebe: The Titan Goddess of Bright Intellect. Mother of Asteria and Leto. Grandmother of Apollo, Artemis, and Hecate. She gifted the gift of prophecy to Apollo. One of the Twelve Titans.

Poseidon: The God of the Sea. Husband of Amphitrite. Son of Rhea and Kronos, brother of Hades and Zeus. One of the Twelve Olympians.

Prometheus: The Titan who formed man from clay. He was punished for giving man divine fire and chained to a rock where a vulture would eat his liver each day but would regenerate each night.

Psyche: The wife of Eros. When people began to boast of her beauty, she angered Aphrodite. Aphrodite sent her son, Eros, to make Psyche fall in love with a monster but Eros fell in love with her.

Rhea: The Titan Goddess of Fertility. Mother of the Olympian Gods. Wife of Kronos who helped to defeat him. One of the Twelve Titans.

Scylla: A sea monster that forms the dangerous straits of Messina with Charybdis. In some myths, she was a nymph transformed into a monster by Poseidon to hide her from his wife's jealousy.

Selene: The Goddess of the Moon. Daughter of Hyperion and sister to Helios (God of the Sun) and Eos (Goddess of the Dawn).

Semele: The Princess of Thebe. Mother of Dionysus. A victim of Hera's trickery, she asked Zeus to show her his true godly form which burned away her life's essence.

Styx: One of the Five Rivers of the Underworld. The River on which oaths are sworn.

Tethys: The Titan Goddess of Fresh Water. Wife of Oceanus. Mother of the Oceanids (Sea nymphs) and River Gods. One of the Twelve Titans.

Theia: The Titan Goddess of Sight. Consort of Hyperion (God of Light). Mother of Selene, Helios, and Eos.

Themis: The Titan Goddess of Divine Law and Order. One of the Twelve Titans.

Theseus: The Hero who slew the Minotaur in the Labyrinth.

Titanides: The Six Original Titan Goddesses.

the Titanomachy: The ten thousand-year war between the Titans and the Olympians. The Titans were defeated and sent to Tartarus and Zeus became King of Olympus.

Typhon: The most fearsome monster in Greek Mythology. Son of Gaea and Tartarus. Husband of Echidna. Created to defeat the Olympian Gods.

Uranus: The Primordial personification of the Sky crafted by Gaea herself. He threw his children, the Cyclopes, and the Hecatoncheires, angering Gaea. Gaea then gave a scythe to Kronos, their youngest son, and told him to castrate Uranus and throw him in Tartarus.

Zeus: The God of the Sky and the King of Olympus. Husband of Hera. Became king after defeating his father in the Titanomachy.

ACKNOWLEDGMENTS

Much Love To:

My mother, who would take me to the library after school and allowed me to grow my love for Greek Mythology.

My father, who always reminds me that I am strong and powerful.

My sister; together, we are going from girls to goddesses.

My Grandparents, who showed me the beautiful legacy that runs through my veins.

My family, who have only shown me love and support.

Malea, for being my best friend and my rock since day one.

Taryn, for growing our love for Greek Mythology together.

Abby, for providing me comfort and smiles on bad days.

Kelsi, for teaching me to reach beyond my comfort zone.

Christina, for always being there for me even when I get crazy.

And, of course, to you, the reader. I hope this adventure through Ancient Greece has allowed you to take a different look at the myths and remind you that; *you were born golden.*

Made in the USA
Monee, IL
20 August 2022